WHY THIS IS AN EASY READER
- This story has been carefully written to keep the young reader's interest high.
- It is told in a simple, open style, with a strong rhythm that adds enjoyment both to reading aloud and silent reading.
- There is a very high percentage of words repeated. It is this skillful repetition which helps the child to read independently. Seeing words again and again, he "practices" the vocabulary he knows, and learns with ease the words that are new.
- Only 72 different words have been used, with plurals and root words counted once.

   Almost one-half of all the words in this story have been used at least three times.

   Almost one-third of all the words in this story have been used at least six times.

   Some words have been used 10, 14 and 17 times.

ABOUT THIS STORY
- Here is a real easy-to-read treat—all the pleasure of a picnic, all the hilarity of funny picnic races, all the pie a young reader can vicariously eat—all told *with only 72 words!* Fun to read—fun to act out.

Hooray for Henry

Story by
JEAN BETHELL

Pictures by
SERGIO LEONE

Editorial Consultant:
LILIAN MOORE

WONDER BOOKS
A Division of Grosset & Dunlap, Inc.
New York, N.Y. 10010

Introduction

These books are meant to help the young reader discover what a delightful experience reading can be. The stories are such fun that they urge the child to try his new reading skills. They are so easy to read that they will encourage and strengthen him as a reader.

The adult will notice that the sentences aren't too long, the words aren't too hard, and the skillful repetition is like a helping hand. What the child will feel is: "This is a good story—and I can read it myself!"

For some children, the best way to meet these stories may be to hear them read aloud at first. Others, who are better prepared to read on their own, may need a little help in the beginning—help that is best given freely. Youngsters who have more experience in reading alone—whether in first or second or third grade—will have the immediate joy of reading "all by myself."

These books have been planned to help all young readers grow—in their pleasure in books and in their power to read them.

Lilian Moore
Specialist in Reading
Formerly of Division of Instructional Research,
New York City Board of Education

© 1966, by Wonder Books,
a Division of Grosset & Dunlap, Inc.
All rights reserved under International and
Pan-American Copyright Conventions.
Published simultaneously in Canada.
Printed in the United States of America.
Library of Congress Catalog Card Number 65-20012

Today is the day
of the big picnic.
Everyone is having fun.

"Say, look at all that food!
Come on, Henry, let's eat."

"Not now. I'm going to
run a race first.
Look at all the prizes!"

This is the water race.

"Run, Henry, run!"

"Faster! FASTER!"

Too fast!

"Come on, Henry, let's eat."

"Not now.

I'm going to run the bag race.

I'm going to win a prize."

This is the bag race.

"One,
two,
three —
go!"

"Hop, Henry, hop!"

"Faster! FASTER!"

Too fast!

No prize for Henry.

"Say, Henry, look at this. Want one?"

"Not now.

I want to win a prize.

I'm going to run the egg race."

This is the egg race.

"One, two, three — go!"

"Run, Henry, run!"

"Faster, FASTER!"

Too fast!

No prize for Henry.

"Here, Henry. Eat this."

"Not now.

I'm going to run the peanut race.

I MUST win a prize!"

This is the peanut race.

"One,
two,
three —
GO!"

"Push, Henry, push!"

"Faster! FASTER!"

Too fast!

No prize for Henry.

"Come on, Henry, let's eat."

"Not now.

I'm going to try the balloon race.

I MUST win a prize."

This is the balloon race!

"One,
two,
three —
BLOW!"

"Blow, Henry, blow!"

"Faster, FASTER!"

Too fast!

No prize for Henry.

"I give up. NOW let's eat."

But now there is nothing to eat.

"No prize.

No food.

What a picnic!

I'm going home."

"One more race!
Come on, everyone!
Get in the pie race!"

"I can't eat a pie."

"We can't eat a pie."

"I can!"

This is the pie race.

"One,

two,

three—

GO!"

"Eat, Henry, eat!"

"Faster! FASTER!"

Hooray for Henry!

He wins the race.

He wins the prize.

"Wow!

What a picnic!"